Date Due

JUL 3 0 1981			
MAR 1 5 1982			
APR 1 1982			
JUL 1 3 1982			
7/22/82			
7-17-84			
APR 2 4 1995			

superstars! superstars! superstars!

CREATIVE EDUCATION SPORTS SUPERSTARS

janetjanetja
lynn lynn l
janetjanetja
lynn lynn ly

janet lynn

by Ann Morse
illustrated by
John Keely

CREATIVE EDUCATION
MANKATO, MINNESOTA

janet lynn

Published by Creative Educational Society, Inc., 123 South Broad Street, Mankato, Minnesota 56001.

Printed in the United States.
Distributed by Childrens Press, 1224 West Van Buren Street, Chicago, Illinois 60607.

Library of Congress Numbers: 75-20355 ISBN: 0-87191-456-5

Library of Congress Cataloging in Publication Data
Morse, Ann. Janet Lynn.
SUMMARY: A biography of the figure skater whose lack of desire to "skate to win" made her decide to turn professional.
1. Lynn, Janet—Juvenile literature. 2. Ice skating—Biography] I. Keely, John. II. Title.
[1. Lynn, Janet. 2. Skating—Juvenile literature.
GV850.L96M67 796.9'1'0924 [B] [92] 75-20355 ISBN 0-87191-456-5

netjanetjane
ynn lynn lyn
netjanetjane
nn lynn lyn

Janet Lynn, world's favorite figure skater, is a radical in the sports world. She doesn't skate to win. She never has.

Janet searches and strives for excellence in her sport. She has yearned for the Olympic gold medal, but her efforts are toward perfection and not toward becoming "better than" someone else. There's the difference; that's what makes Janet Lynn a radical.

"Don't get me wrong," Janet says. "I believe in setting goals. That's the only way to bring the best out of yourself. But winning isn't everything. You can't make that your whole life and call yourself worthless if you don't reach your goal."

When Janet Lynn smiles on the ice, it is a genuine expression of what she feels inside. She feels that she can't become so concerned about winning that she begins to dislike her competitors. "All kinds of ugly things happen when I start trying to beat," Janet said. "And besides that, it doesn't bring out my best skating – just the opposite. I've proved that over and over."

Though a five-time winner in the figure skating

nationals and an Olympic medalist, Janet Lynn has experienced many losses. She approaches skating realistically, so that skating, not winning, has been her life for more than 20 years. "Maybe if I'd started thinking about winning when I was young, I could have made myself want to win so badly I could have done it. But I wouldn't have been genuine."

A different spirit set aflame the two-and-a-half-year-old toddler. Born Janet Lynn Nowicki on April 6, 1953, Janet began skating just two years later. The spirit of challenge set the chunky little girl twirling and tumbling on the ice. And the child's spirit of determination told the rest of the Nowicki family not to help its youngest member up.

Florian Nowicki thought nothing of taking his tiny daughter along to the skating pond, with his two sons, Larry and Glenn, and their Cub Scout troop. "And, do you know, before we knew what happened," her father said, "that little girl had taught herself to skate backward?"

At an early age, Janet grabbed hold of skating. But it was not so easy to break away from the hold shyness had on her. Ethelyne Nowicki quickly put her daughter in skating classes to help her overcome shyness.

At three and a half, Janet skated better than many teen-agers in her class at the Michael Kirby Ice Skating

School. When her teacher asked all the students to write a report on the things they had learned, she had to express herself in pictures. Preschooler Janet had not yet learned to write.

The very thought of anyone – parents, teacher, friends – watching her made Janet want to skate perfectly. Shortly after her fourth birthday, Janet and the other students at the Michael Kirby Ice Skating School prepared for an Ice Carnival at the end of the season. When a few parents and friends gathered at the large Chicago Stadium, Janet took one look at that rink, home of the Black Hawks, and started sobbing. Her little friend Debby dragged Janet onto the ice, and she soon forgot her fear. Janet Lynn's performing career was off to a gliding start.

By five Janet entered two new "schools": Kindergarten at Central School in Chicago and a difficult phase in skating called school (or compulsory) figures. School figures brought to Janet frustrations and challenges which would remain throughout her skating career.

These figures are 70 variations on the figure eight. Skaters have to learn them in order to pass the eight official tests of the United States Figure Skating Association (USFSA). It is important to trace a perfect mark on the ice and then re-trace the same figure many times. It is upon those traces, or marks, on the ice that judges score.

When she was nearly six, Janet performed solo at another of the school's Ice Carnivals. It was a memorable time for her because it was the last time her Grandmother Gehrke saw her skate. Two months later she died, and Janet's grandfather moved in with the Nowicki family.

Once Janet started taking private skating lessons, her patch (time to practice figures on a small square or "patch") was from 5 to 6 a.m. on Saturdays. That meant getting up at 3 a.m. in order to reach the rink on the other side of Chicago by five. But as her mother once said to a reporter, "What do you do when all a little girl says is, 'I wanna skate, I wanna skate'."

The Nowickis helped, struggled, sacrificed; but they never pushed Janet along the disciplined path of figure skating. They have said that they realized her talent and sought to help her express it.

It wasn't long before Florian and Ethelyne Nowicki noticed that Janet was outgrowing Chicago's figure skating teachers. They had heard of the excellent skaters and teachers at the Wagon Wheel in Rockton, Illinois, about 100 miles north of Chicago. One August morning in 1959, the Nowicki family visited the famous resort. The rustic buildings constructed from logs fascinated the children. They swam, bowled, watched the candy kitchen, and finally went skating.

Janet remembers being overwhelmed by the young, vibrant skater whose students seemed to be totally absorbed in what she was saying. Janet's mother and father were attracted to her, too. Before she knew it, her parents were getting acquainted with Slavka Kohout (pronounced "ka-*hoot*"), junior ladies national runner-up in 1946 and now manager and resident professional of the Wagon Wheel Ice Palace.

Watching little Janet skate, Slavka Kohout eagerly accepted the invitation to give her a short lesson. Teacher and student spent only 15 minutes together, jumping, waltzing, doing three-turns and single jumps. "But when she talked," Janet said of her teacher recently, "she had so much meaning in her voice. I've never been so captivated in my life." The quarter-hour lesson was the beginning of the athlete's long, arduous, up-hill struggle and the end of the Nowicki's search for a teacher.

Janet wonders now if her parents gasped when Slavka Kohout suggested she come to the Wagon Wheel twice a week for lessons. Inconvenience or not, the Nowickis chose Wednesdays and Saturdays, and Mrs. Nowicki quickly obtained permission for Janet to miss Wednesdays during her first grade year at school.

Every Tuesday afternoon Mrs. Nowicki and Janet would drive the 100 miles to the Wagon Wheel, Janet would skate in the evening and all the next day, and they'd drive back Wednesday night. The whole family made the trip every Friday evening and wouldn't return until Sunday night. Florian Nowicki, a pharmacist who owned a drug store in Chicago, frequently worked on the weekends at a store near the Wagon Wheel. Even in blizzards when many local skaters

didn't make it, the Nowicki family always made the trip.

During her first year Janet passed both the preliminary and the first of the USFSA's eight tests. Janet says these tests were the only goal her parents suggested she make for herself. But they did not force her. Janet is sure now that they must have dreaded that long trip twice each week, but they never showed any resistance. Mr. and Mrs. Nowicki didn't show any resistance either when Slavka Kohout suggested that for simplicity Janet drop her last name in skating competitions. Hence, Janet Lynn.

Summer brought an end to the constant travel. Janet, her mother, and her younger sister Carol moved to the Wagon Wheel for the summer. Her father, brothers, and grandfather ran the store and the house in Chicago and frequently fished the trout streams in Wisconsin.

Being on the ice every day, Janet progressed rapidly. By the end of the summer she passed USFSA Test number two and returned to Chicago for school.

Janet barely had her things settled in her second-grade desk when Slavka Kohout felt another change had to be made. "Look, if you want Janet to keep going in skating," she told the Nowickis, "we're just going to have to work out something for her to skate every day." Feeling that two lessons a week kept Janet at a standstill, the teacher wanted to arrange for her to live nearby with another skater's family. Her parents agreed, and by October Janet was living with Jada Steinke's family.

Jada was four years older than Janet, but they still enjoyed sharing skating experiences with one another. At night, however, after the lights were off and Jada was asleep, seven-year-old Janet was lonesome. She would see her family every weekend, but that wasn't enough. Realizing Janet's homesickness, her family soon made another change. Grandpa Gehrke moved to Rockton to take care of Janet. The two rented an apartment, and Janet felt secure. Though her pony tail wouldn't be brushed and re-tied for weeks at a time, grandfather and granddaughter enjoyed each other's company.

By New Year's, Janet was ready for her first competition – the Midwestern subsectional in Troy, Ohio. She had worked long hours on the hardest part – the school figures. At that time, the figures comprised 60 percent of the score. Janet and her teacher had also put together a free-skating program, a ballet-like performance set to music. Even at seven, Janet excelled in free skating; she felt a kind of magic take over when her feet left the ice in a spin or jump.

Out of 20, Janet took thirteenth place in the school figures. She was crushed. Only the first eight could go on to the free-skating program. Janet hated the school figures, but after the Troy competition she made up her mind that she would never again be stopped from doing her free-skating program. Whether the compulsory figures made sense to her or not, she decided she would try to find them interesting.

As Janet moved into third grade and into the world of frequent competition, her family moved to Rockford, Illinois, (about 15 miles from the Wagon Wheel). Florian Nowicki sold his drug store in Chicago and was able to manage one in Rockford. It would be seven years before he was able to buy a store again. But these were sacrifices both he and his wife made willingly in the light of Janet's talent.

Meanwhile Janet was adding new words to her vocabulary – *subsectionals* (competition within one region; Janet was in the Upper Great Lakes subsectional), *sectionals* (competitions in the East, Midwest, and West), *nationals* (in which champions of each division and of the entire nation are determined), and *worlds* (competitions held usually in Europe, or North America). Two other side competitions were the *North Americans* (held every odd-numbered year right after the Nationals) and the *Winter Olympics* (held every four years).

When Janet was 8, she and the other skaters at Wagon

Wheel were hosts for the subsectionals. Keeping her promise to herself, Janet placed fourth in the school figures and so went on to do her free-skating program. She knew she had done well, but astonished herself when she learned she had placed first in the overall competition.

Slavka Kohout continued to put Janet through a rigorous pace. The teacher wanted Janet to move along with the USFSA tests so that she could enter junior and senior divisions in just a few years. By nine, Janet not only passed her fifth USFSA test and competed in the junior division in the subsectionals, but she also took first place.

At the sectionals in Sioux City, she placed third and so was eligible for the nationals in Long Beach, California. There the youngest entrant came in eleventh – last place. Far from disappointed, Janet just let the experience settle and went on to the exhibitions and invitationals Miss Kohout had planned for her.

Because Janet showed such refined talent at a very young age, little was left to chance in her life. Her skating ability determined what she would do with most of her time. One writer even said that "Janet is deeply religious, the natural result perhaps of a childhood deprived of the haphazard." No one knows exactly what makes a person religious, but Janet has said that her religious beliefs have given

her great comfort as well as determination in her skating career.

Janet continued to whip along through the USFSA tests. On August 29, 1964, she passed test number eight and received a gold medal and papers complimenting her on being the youngest person to complete all the tests.

At Lincoln Junior High School, Janet was able to

arrange her schedule so that she could skate from seven until ten every morning and then go to school. Of course there would be more skating after school and all day Saturday. One of her teachers, Robert Winters, said, "Janet was the same in school as she was in her skating. She settled only for perfection."

At 12, Janet's teachers let her take two weeks off to prepare for the 1966 nationals in Berkeley, California. During the year she had been working on the triple salchow (a backward takeoff, three complete turns in the air, and a backward landing). During the practice for the nationals, however, skating experts advised Slavka Kohout against letting Janet try it in competition.

When it came time for her free-skating program, Janet breezed onto the ice and zipped into the triple salchow and – to her surprise – landed it! Grinning from ear to ear, Janet said she could have skated all night after that. A half hour later, she waited in the press room for the results. When a reporter told Janet she had just won the nationals, she burst into tears. She had never even placed first in a sectional competition, let alone nationals!

The national champion went home to exams and to winning a place on the honor roll at school. The kids at school liked Janet. She tried not to let her skating talents stand in the way of friendship. Still, it was hard.

Later, when Janet was dating, she asked a boy to a Sadie Hawkins dance. When they arrived at the dance, Janet greeted her friends nervously. She wondered how to tell her date that she had to leave in 15 minutes to get enough sleep for a long practice session the next day. Janet wanted desperately to be "in" with the kids, but she had also set some skating goals. She decided to stay with those goals even when they hurt.

After the nationals in Berkeley, Slavka Kohout wanted Janet to get some experience in international competition. In the spring of 1966, Janet entered the competition at Oberstdorf, Germany. She placed second, and the experience boosted her confidence. She and Slavka also traveled to the figure skating capital of the world – Davos, Switzerland.

Returning to Rockford, Illinois, Janet had to struggle again to be "in" with the kids. Rockford, not Europe, interested most of her friends. That was when Janet decided she had to feel comfortable with who she was and what she was doing, and not try to be like anyone else.

As the 1968 Olympics neared, school schedules were rearranged. Janet completed most of her ninth grade in the first semester. After subsectionals and sectionals, Janet was ready for the nationals in Philadelphia in January, 1968.

"It was cold, damp, and very, very dark here Friday morning," one reporter wrote, "when Janet Lynn walked down the steps of the Belvue-Stratford Hotel. Skating began at 7 a.m. This was her bid for the United States Olympic Team."

Very few people show up for the compulsory figures.

There is no music, no glamour. It is a task to be completed and judged. Between figures, Janet would slip into a coat and wait on the bleachers with her mother and Slavka Kohout. Now and then she would take a drink of a quick-energy formula her pharmacist father had prepared.

Finishing fourth in a field of 12, Janet breathed a sigh of relief. With the compulsory figures behind her, she knew she still had a good chance of becoming one of the youngest Olympic team members.

Or would she? Her chances seemed to dim when she fell on the triple salchow and again on the double lutz in her free skating. Judges are not supposed to count falls, only what the skater is able to complete. But even objective judges can hardly overlook two falls.

Yet in spite of her falls, Janet moved into third place in the nationals and so moved onto the United States Olympic Team. Nineteen-year-old Peggy Fleming, twenty-year-old Tina Noyes, and fourteen-year-old Janet Lynn would be representing the United States at the Tenth Winter Olympics in Grenoble, France.

Grenoble was an awesome experience for the youngest United States skater. Fog hovered over the mountainous town in France, and Janet could feel the damp chill in her bones. Flu invaded Olympic Village and struck Janet along with many other athletes. The doctor told Janet not to march in the opening ceremonies. "But there was *no way* I was going to miss that experience," Janet said. "It was one of the truly thrilling times of my life to march into that arena behind the flag of my country."

One of Rockford's newspaper reporters who had been writing several stories on Janet called Grenoble to find out how Janet was doing. Slavka Kohout told him she was doing pretty well but missed American hamburgers. Before she knew it, McDonalds had heard about it and had put 30 pounds of hamburger, buns, catsup, mustard, and pickles on an Air France headed for Grenoble. All 119 members of the United States team shared in the little bit of home.

During the compulsory figures, Janet really felt the effects of the flu. She placed fourteenth among 32 skaters. But she felt better the day of her free skating and repeated the program she had done in Philadelphia, minus the falls. In free skating she placed sixth and ninth overall. Peggy Fleming, of course, took the only gold medal for the United States.

The excitement was not yet over. Janet left Grenoble immediately for Geneva, Switzerland, for the worlds competition. Not only had she taken her flu with her, but, when she arrived in Geneva, it had turned into strep throat. She isn't sure how she survived the school figures, but at the end she placed ninth.

A thousand people must have been waiting at the Rockford airport when Janet Lynn flew home that windy March day. "Oh no –" Janet exclaimed as she looked out the plane window, "I think I'll sleep in the plane tonight." The mayor had proclaimed a Janet Lynn Day. Janet, Rockford's young heroine, rode on the city's newest fire truck in a motorcade through town. Signs and streamers decorated the outside and inside of the Nowicki house. A tired, happy, and overwhelmed young skater fell into bed that night and slept through the cleanup the next day.

Two days later the Olympics were far away. Janet was back at Lincoln Junior High catching up on schoolwork, friendships, and everyday routine.

Since Janet had progressed as far as the world competition, she didn't have to go through subsectionals and sectionals the next year. So after ten months without any competition, Janet went right into the 1969 nationals in Seattle, Washington. That year figures and free skating were counted on a 50-50 basis instead of 60-40 – a change Janet appreciated. By the end of both parts of the competition, there was only a .59 difference in the scoring of the three skaters: Tina Noyes, Julie Holmes and Janet. Though Tina was the favored one to take the nationals, the trophy fell to an ecstatic Janet.

She had little time to relax in her victory; for the North Americans were the following week in Oakland, California. Karen Magnussen, Janet's chief rival from Canada, had just suffered defeat; so she came charging into the North Americans with a tough spirit. Karen led on the school figures, and the free-skating competition seemed close. Janet and Karen waited together for the final scores. "Congratulations," Janet whispered to Karen as she felt sure Karen would take the title. "Not yet," Karen responded nervously. All of a sudden, Peggy Fleming was handing Janet Lynn the big silver bowl. With 1.4 points difference, Janet had never had such a close win.

This time all the Rockford fans drove to Chicago's O'Hare airport to welcome their star. About forty of Janet's friends from Guilford High School had used 80 rolls of toilet paper to decorate the Nowicki house, trees, bushes; and a maze of string in her bedroom doorway tangled Janet in a web of victory.

Confidence turned to nervousness, however, when, only two weeks later, Janet faced the best skaters for the worlds competition in Colorado Springs, Colorado. Disappointedly, Janet ended up fifth; she knew she could have skated better. But after the worlds, the top skaters put on an exhibition tour. Janet loved the experience – she could relax and get to know the other skaters in a way not possible during competition. As she said, "It was another rare chance to be real with people."

And so Janet Lynn's record goes: At 16, she was first in the U.S. and sixth in the world. She was first in the U.S. and fourth in the world at 17. And in 1972 she was once more first in the U.S. Then came practice for the Winter Olympics in Sapporo, Japan.

Slavka Kohout arranged for the French skating expert Pierre Brunet to help Janet with school figures. Brunet, a genius of a skater himself and a brilliant mentor of world champions, worked patiently and steadily with Janet.

"I do not think there is any other sport so difficult as figure skating. Average human beings cannot do it," says Brunet. He feels that it is the one complete sport because it requires equilibrium, perfect ambidexterity, and a combination of strength and beauty. "You have to be able to spin like a top without falling and yet be athletic enough to jump like a gazelle and land on one foot and not fall."

Janet would have the chance to prove her strength and beauty in Japan. Sapporo nestles in Japan's northernmost island called Hokkaido. White with snow, the town appeared exquisite to Janet. More mature and minus the flu, Janet found the opening ceremonies in Sapporo more thrilling than in Grenoble.

The ceremonies quickly faded into hard work. The ladies figure skating was scheduled early. On the first day Janet executed three figures in good form and placed third. However, the next day, on a change loop, she fell apart and went down to fourth place. A shattered Janet dodged reporters, as she tried to hide her tears and run back to her room. Slavka Kohout and Janet's mother comforted her. But in time, it was Janet who calmed and relaxed herself. She said she did it through prayer. Having the whole next day before the night competition, Janet felt renewed and ready for anything.

Janet's performance in free skating that night was pure artistry. A reporter for the *London Observer* wrote, "Her performance here was one of those rare occasions when sport is lifted into the realms of art. . . . when she moves backwards and her arms are outstretched, she is indeed a young girl in love with the world."

Suddenly, Janet jarred the spectators back down to earth when her flying sit-spin brought her down on the ice. "I guess the whole world groaned when I fell," Janet said later. But at the moment Janet didn't have time to groan. She hopped up, went into the double axle, and finished out the rest of her program with the same smile on her face.

When her points were tallied, Janet received seven 5.7s and two 5.8s for technical merit. For artistic impression she received six 5.9s and two 5.8s and a perfect 6.0 from the judge who had been toughest on her in the school figures. When all the points were totaled, Janet took third. "I stood there on the awards stand," Janet said, "and was nothing but happy as I accepted my huge two-inch bronze medal."

To the Japanese, though, it was as if Janet had turned bronze into gold, so captivated were they by her charm. Her room in Olympia Village was overflowing with fan mail. One of her friends suggested she sign her name on the wall, figuring the Village would be repainted anyway. So when they left, Janet took a felt-tip pen and scrawled "Peace + Love! Janet Lynn USA 1972 Ladies Figure Skating 3rd Place." Later, when the Village was turned into apartments, there was discussion about keeping Janet Lynn's farewell sign. The family moving in wanted it left, except the mother who finally gave in under pressure.

At home, being the object of so much attention was again overwhelming to Janet. But the one place where she could skate and be herself was the Wagon Wheel rink. Slavka

Kohout saw to that. She never allowed skaters to make a fuss over Janet. It became a second home.

One summer day following the Olympics, Janet went to the rink for an afternoon of practice. But after 10 minutes, she returned home. "Mom, I can't do it," Janet said. She was tired of skating; it bored and depressed her. She talked with her parents, her brothers, her teacher, her pastor. Together she and they decided to stay with skating for another year.

Janet said she felt God wanted her to skate another year. But it wasn't easy to overcome the tediousness. Also, Janet had to struggle with a recurring weight problem. With extra weight, she knew she wasn't skating as well, and she knew others were noticing it, too.

At the 1973 nationals in Minneapolis, Minnesota, everyone expected Janet to do even better because school figures now counted 40 percent; a compulsory short program with music was added for 20 percent; and the regular free-skating program was 40 percent. But despite the scoring change and the extra help from Pierre Brunet, Janet placed second in both the school figures and the short compulsory program. But the next night Janet skated a perfect free-skating program and took the nationals for the fifth time in a row.

Slavka Kohout felt 1973 would be Janet's year. "Until now, Janet wasn't really ready. This is the first year she is really a top world competitor. She's emotionally and mentally mature. She wasn't quite before." Slavka Kohout was speaking with reporters before the worlds in Bratislava, Czechoslovakia. It was a sure bet for Janet to take the worlds championship for the first time.

It was cold the day of the school figures competition

in Bratislava. But Janet managed to skate a close second behind Karen Magnussen. The next day, when the short compulsory program was scheduled, it seemed even colder. Janet felt her legs tense as she started off with a shaky spin. She had planned a double axle/double toe loop. But she fell at the start of the combination and then again on the last axle. Two falls within two minutes!

Both she and Slavka burst into tears as soon as they reached the dressing room. Even Janet's rival, Karen Magnussen, was stunned. She kept repeating, "I can't believe it . . . Janet, I never wanted you to skate like that." Janet ended twelfth in that competition. It was indeed the hardest year of her life.

Despite her dislike for school figures, observers felt that Janet would have won had she not fallen. "I'm not conscious of trying to smile," she says. "When I didn't win at Bratislava, I was disappointed; but I still wanted to do the best I could."

Not long after the 1973 international competition, Janet Lynn announced her decision to go professional. She wasn't quitting skating; she was entering a new phase. Janet said she was happy she had "gutted it out" through a difficult year. "It was just that I got tired of competing. After fourteen years of serious competition, I was bored and depressed.

Something always seemed to happen when I was on the verge of winning." So on June 19, 1973, Janet Lynn signed contracts that will pay her more than $2 million. One contract with the Ice Follies will pay her $1.4 million over three years; the other contract covers television specials and a motion picture.

Janet is happy to be able to earn the money. It helps to repay her parents, and she feels the money helps her to aid less fortunate people through worthwhile projects.

Now Janet performs more than she practices. She has more time for church work and speaking engagements. She has even written a book, *Peace + Love,* which describes her skating career and religious beliefs. "I don't have to beat anyone but myself," she says now. Still, Janet did take time out to go and capture the World's Professional Women's Championship title in Tokyo, Japan, in 1974.

Janet says she loves performing. "I have to watch my timing. But I love putting my feelings to music." Janet's feelings are maturing as she matures. On the Ice Follies' playbills, she is called "America's Sweetheart" or "Pixie Princess." She has captured attention with her winning smile and graceful manner. But Janet Lynn is more than the labels. She is a strong, disciplined skater with a sense of *search* about her life.

superstars! superstars! superstars!

CREATIVE EDUCATION SPORTS SUPERSTARS

JACKIE ROBINSON
MUHAMMAD ALI
O. J. SIMPSON
JOHNNY BENCH
WILT CHAMBERLAIN
ARNOLD PALMER
A. J. FOYT
JOHNNY UNITAS
GORDIE HOWE
WALT FRAZIER
PHIL AND TONY ESPOSITO
BOB GRIESE

JACK NICKLAUS
BILL RUSSELL
MARK SPITZ
VINCE LOMBARDI
BILLIE JEAN KING
ROBERTO CLEMENTE
JOE NAMATH
BOBBY HULL
HANK AARON
JERRY WEST
TOM SEAVER

FRANK ROBINSON
PANCHO GONZALES
LEE TREVINO
KAREEM ABDUL JABBAR
JEAN CLAUDE KILLY
EVONNE GOOLAGONG
ARTHUR ASHE
SECRETARIAT
ROGER STAUBACH
FRAN TARKENTON
BOBBY ORR
LARRY CSONKA
JOHNNY MILLER
FRANCO HARRIS

BILL WALTON
ALAN PAGE
PEGGY FLEMING
OLGA KORBUT
DON SCHULA
MICKEY MANTLE
EVEL KNIEVEL
JIMMY CONNORS
CHRIS EVERT
PETER REVSON
KATHY WHITWORTH
JACKIE STEWART
STAN SMITH
JANET LYNN